Daffodils & Other Poems

A collection of nature inspired and
motivational poems.

Vasu Gangapalli

Made with ❤ on the BookLeaf Publishing Platform
www.bookleafpub.in
www.bookleafpub.com

Dedication

This poetry collection is dedicated to my dear friend Mantu (Ruby Sarkar). One day, I found her hobbies and contact details listed on the penpals column in the national newspaper The Asian Age. I decided to write my first letter to her seeking her valuable friendship. My heart never knew such a joy when I got reply from her accepting my friendship. We started as pen friends exchanging letters during our college days.

Then became Orkut and Facebook friends. I travelled in flight for the first time in life to meet her at her place. There was turbulence due to bad weather while I was about to reach her city due to a Strom that was about to hit her city, fortunately the Strom took a diversion and went to some other place. I landed safely and spent next few days in her wonderful company. Those were some of the best and memorable days of my life. I was reading Chetan Bhagat's book One Night at a Call Centre during the journey. I had my Sony Ericson K710i mobile that just had 2 megapixel camera, but shot some amazing pictures then.

Preface

Poetry has always been my sanctuary—a place where thoughts find rhythm, where silence speaks, and where emotions bloom into words. *"Daffodils & Other Poems"* is not just a collection of verses; it is a journey through nature's quiet wisdom and the unwavering spirit of human resilience.

Growing up, I often found solace in the rustling leaves, the whispering winds, and the endless sky that stretched beyond horizons. Nature, in its quiet yet powerful way, became my greatest muse. Each sunrise reminded me of new beginnings, and each fallen leaf taught me that change is inevitable, yet beautiful. Through these poems, I have tried to capture those fleeting moments—the ones we often overlook but carry the deepest meanings.

Beyond nature, this collection

also embraces the spirit of motivation. Life has its share of storms, but within us lies the strength to weather them. As someone who has walked the path of literature with a dream of reaching hearts across the world, I have learned that perseverance is poetry in itself. Every challenge is a stanza, every triumph a rhyme, and every setback a pause that makes the next line even more powerful.

I hope these words bring you the

same sense of peace, courage,
and inspiration that they brought
me while writing them. May they
remind you to find beauty in the
smallest moments and strength
in the quietest whispers of life.

Vasu Gangapalli

Acknowledgements

Poetry found me in the quiet corners of my childhood, where the verses of great poets became my earliest companions. I owe my deepest gratitude to the literary giants who first stirred my soul—William Blake, with his visionary lines; William Wordsworth, whose nature poetry taught me to see the world with wonder; Rabindranath Tagore, whose wisdom echoed in my thoughts; and John Keats, whose odes breathed life into emotions. Their words were more than ink on pages; they were whispers of inspiration that led me to try my own poetry, to mold my emotions into verse, and to believe in the power of expression.

To my family, who nurtured my love for words, and to my friends who encouraged me even when my first attempts were hesitant, thank you for your unwavering support. To every reader who finds a moment of reflection, solace, or inspiration in these pages, this book belongs as much to you as it does to me.

Finally, I extend my gratitude to the unseen forces of nature and life itself—each sunrise, each falling leaf, each whispered breeze—that continue to inspire and shape my poetry. May this book be a tribute to all that is beautiful, fleeting, and eternal in the world around us.

Vasu Gangapalli

1. Why I can't be?

A Poem

One evening I was depressed,
And was walking in a lonely path
Suddenly, the wind blew up the
dry
Leaves fallen on the ground
Swirled and took them to the sky

It was magic and wonderful
Seeing the dry leaves dancing
In front of my eyes
Then a thought crossed my mind
Why can't I be like the wind,

Which had lifted the fallen
Leaves from the ground
And made them to touch the sky!

Why can't I help those who have
Fallen from the grace,
Those who have failed
And those who are left behind,
Help them to find their lost hope
And bring back the smile to their
face.

2. Bird's Song

A Poem

You sing so softly yet so clear,
Your song rhymes without a
word.
Your Beautiful song travels along
with the cool and gentle breeze
Reaches the nearby stream,
Adds to its flowing icy cold
waters
Which adds music to your song
While passing through the
Crevices of the rocks.

Then your song reaches
the wonderful mountains
Passing through bushes and
trees.
As the sun's rays pierces through
The sleepy dark skies,
Into the greenery,
Into the clear water stream
Sending the owl and bats
back to sleep.

While your wonderful song
soothes
And wakes up Mother Nature
Like some beautiful wake up
song!

3. Climb a Mountain

A Poem

I'd like to climb a mountain,
While the moon lights up the
way
As my heart overflows with joy
Like a fountain
Seeing millions of stars
Shining in the sky!

I'd then sit on some rock,
While the gentle breeze
It wipes my sweat away
I set free the horses

Of worries from the staple
Of my mind
As my shadow gives me
Company from behind

The owl hoots from the branch
Of some nearby trees,
As the grass blades are under
My feet try to tickle me
Bats fly as high as the moon,
Which I can see

My heart is soothed in this
Tranquil night,
Listening to the song of
Crickets from nearby bush

I've whole night with me
And there is nowhere to rush

4. A Cup of Tea

A Poem

I stand still waiting
for my cup of tea,
As the tea maker
 brews it for me.

 A hundred thoughts
running in my mind
like the sea,
Whereas my face would
appear as tranquil
as it could be.

As the wonderful smell
spreads through the air,
Some people are here
to discuss things and
their thoughts to share.

As the first sip touches
my tongue and taste
registers in my brain,
I forget all my worries
and my troubled heart: its strain.

Whenever I would like
to pause for a moment
and set my thoughts free,
It is here I halt to have

my cup of tea
as the surroundings my camera
like eyes focus to see.

5. Have Faith

A Poem

Have faith firm
In your heart,
As the day will
Surely come.

Sleep peacefully
Like a bud,
Expecting to open
Its heart to the
The first ray of dawn.

Your sufferings are

Like the dark clouds
In the sky,
But the rays of light
Will surely pierces
Through it and
Light the gloomy path.
Now, silence is
Preparing for the
Voice of joy.

Have Faith,
It'll surely happen
Like the seed
In the deep soil,
Which will surely sprout,

Become a plant
And then a tree.

6. Stargazing

A Poem

I would like to drive with my dog
To some unknown serene place,
When the stars are shining in
The sky is so bright.

No other vehicle is behind me.
To race;
While the path is illuminated
With the full moonlight.
I stop by some vast green
grassland,
Lay down on the ground;

And rest my head on my hand.
And listen to the crickets' sound.

The sky is charcoal black,
Spread across the blanket
Of stars quite far,
The silence brings joy to my
heart
And peace to my mind.

I can make my objects with the
Twinkling stars spread
Across the skies,
Occasionally, witnessing the
Dance of the fireflies.

I then close my eyes to wander

In my dream,
While listening to the melodious
Music coming from a nearby
stream.

Then I lie down on the
Grass bed,
And let my mind wander
Into the dreamland's bed
Until the sun kisses my
Forehead and wakes
Me up again!

7. The Gulmohar Tree

A poem

My heart fills with immense joy.
Whenever I see,
A full-bloom Gulmohar tree.
I eagerly wait for May
Every year,
To have a glimpse of my
favourite
Tree on a bright sunny day,
I wonder how majestic it does
Appear,
With its slender leaves of
Mesmerizing green

Bright red petals of the
Peacock flower
That adds sheer beauty that
Could be seen
It's breathtaking even to see
Them from any tall tower
Dressed in their beautiful
Summer attire,
I get a feeling all these
Wonderful trees are on fire!

8. A Candle

A Poem

I would like to get my
Inspiration from
A burning candle,
Which stands brave
Against the
Fighting wind,
It melts down
Itself with the
Burning flame
Above,
To provide us
Some brightness

In the room filled
With darkness.
It finds its joy
In sharing its flame
With fellow candle
To increase the
Brightness and to
Drive the creepy
Darkness away.

9. One Rainy Day

A Poem

I woke up from sleep one
Rainy day,
When the sun was hidden
Beneath the clouds
Of darkest grey.

The falling rain made
the wonderful
Pitter-patter sound,
I saw some kids hop
And skip in puddles
Of rainwater on the ground.

A little bird was perched.

On a telephone wire,
A little boy completely
Drenched ran behind
A rolling tyre.
I tried to catch the rain.

Drops falling on my
Window sill,
When the cool breeze
Embraced me with
An icy chill.

Come drizzling rain;
Once again,
So that I could forget

At least for that moment

All my pain.

10. Morning

A Poem

When the sun rises to light,
The sky, with its rays
That not only makes things
bright,
It also gives colours to nature,
like
A painter always does.

When the entire surrounding
view,
It is captured within a drop of
dew

People start waking up one by
one,
Some with a stretch and
Some with a yawn

When the birds rise and chirp,
Welcoming the new day
The gentle breeze touching,
Everything, including the wavy
lawn

The playful squirrels running
Up a shady tree,
While a beautiful flower attracts
A buzzing bee
The morning provides more

beauty

Then eyes can see!

11. Determination

A Poem

It's like that one drop
of a flowing river
That leaps and lands
on the green grass

Beside the flowing river
Unlike the millions
of drops that continue to
Flow along with the stream

If we are determined
Then, we can change

The course of our destiny
It's like the glove of
The boxer in the ring

Though having taken
Much beating
Yet, it comes forward
To strike the opponent
If determination sets
in one's mind
Then, even a loser can win.

12. Winter and Fire

A Poem

In the winter's grasp, I wandered
alone,
A heart encased in ice, chilled to
the bone.
The winds whispered fear, the
snow froze my tears,
Frozen in silence, bound by my
own fears.

The cold was a cloak that I wore
every day,
A shield from the world, keeping

warmth at bay.
Loneliness always echoed in the
hollow heart inside,
I ended up being a frostbitten
soul, nowhere to hide.

But then, like a flicker or a spark,
a bright glow,
A flame that danced where the
cold winds blew.
Fire, so fierce, began to ignite,
Melting the shadows away into
dark, restoring the light.

With each breath, the embers
grew bright,

Warming my fingers that had
trembled in night.
It brought back the warmth of
care, it hummed with hope,
A beacon of strength that helped
me to cope.

The fire was more than just heat
to my cold skin,
It was courage that was reborn,
a warmth in my little heart's
deep within.
Resilience kindled where frost
had once lain,
A fire that burned through the
echoes

of silence suffering and pain.

Now winter may come, with its
chill and its bite,
But fire within me that rekindles
courage
will keep the night bright.
For I've learned that both cold
and flame must be,
To know what it means to be
truly free.

13. December

A Poem

It's so cold outside,
With snow covered
Almost everywhere.

With Christmas trees
Decorated with stars,
Bells and other pretty
Things.
The pleasant sound of
The jingle bells.

America looks its best

During this time of
The year.
I like December,
It makes me to
Remember the events
For the whole year,
Some memorable,
Some have already forgotten.

I like December,
As it brings Christmas,
Also, at the end of the year,
And heralds a new year.

14. We All Grew Up

A Poem

We all grew up in the blink of an
eye,
From chasing dreams beneath the
sky.
From laughter echoing down the
street,
To busy lives with goals to meet.

We all grew up, though it felt so
fast,
Moments of childhood now
shadows cast.

Once carefree hearts now weigh
the load,
Walking alone on a winding
road.

We all grew up, but left behind,
Pieces of innocence, moments
unkind.
Paper boats, and secret plans,
Fading with time like shifting
sands.
We all grew up, but still we
yearn,
For the days with no lessons to
learn.

The scrape of knees, the taste of
rain,
Memories sweet, mingled with
pain.
We all grew up, yet deep inside,
A child still dwells where dreams
reside.

A spark of wonder, a sense of
play,
Reminds us of who we were that
day.
We all grew up, but the ties
remain,
Woven with love, through joy
and pain.

Though paths may part, and
years may flee,
We carry our youth in our
history.

15. Don't Give Up!

A Poem

Sorrows, pain and failure
could you give us a painful pinch,
Let's stand tall and fight
and they will vanish inch by
inch.

Let us wake up with this
new determination every dawn.
Let's not worry about past things
now and have gone.

Like every gloominess of the

grey,
Certainly, has the dawn
of the brightest day.
Hard work is the grain that
grows in the
life's field,
Success is its fruit which yields.

Let us not give up in this
moment and rest,
Let us try one more time with
our effort of the best,
As life is throwing in new
challenges
at us to test.

It is courage and determination
we need to cross this,
Hurdle in life, and God is surely
there for us to bless.

16. Fireside Fables

A Poem

Gather around the ember's glow,
Where ancient tales and whispers flow.
The fire crackles, the shadows dance,
In flickering light, we fall to trance.

The storyteller clears his throat,
His voice a ship, his words a boat.
Across the seas of time we all

sail,
Through every myth and
weathered tale.

Of heroes bold and spirits bright,
Of witches cackling in the night.
Of lovers lost and kingdoms torn,
Of cursed crowns and roses
worn.

The flames leap high with each
new plot,
The world beyond is soon forgot.
For in this glow, both young and
old,
Find warmth in stories centuries

told.

Oh, fireside fables, old and true,
Your magic binds us, through and
through.
When embers fade and night
grows deep,
Your whispered secrets softly
sleep.

But when the logs are stacked
anew,
And flames return in golden hue,
The fables rise, the voices call,
And we are bound in tales once
more.

17. Daffodils

A Poem

Like some mesmerizing beauty
Hidden beneath the parting mist,
I had seen them in my dream
One night,
Beside a running stream

With so many colours of nature
To make my humble soul bright!
I saw them swaying with a
A couple of buzzing bees,

Beneath the trees,

On whose branches Orioles
Sang a melodious song,
This is where I felt,
My little heart would genuinely
belong.

With a gentle breeze,
Swinging them along with green
Grass blades drenched with
Some dew,
I could recall wonderful moments
There were only a few like this.

I had a joyful tear in my eye,
Then I realized that I could die
A thousand deaths to spend

A few moments with my
Beautiful and wonderful-
Daffodils!

18. Spring Morning

A Poem

One spring morning, I went for a
walk,
With plants, trees, and bushes
spread
Across my way.

I could hear the birds chirp.
And mother nature talk;
It was going to be another
Beautiful day!

The first rays of the sunlit

The dark sky,
Birds left their nests and
I began to fly.

I could hear the buzzing of
The bees,
And Cuckoos sing in unison
From some branches of trees.
I listened to the sound of
a flowing stream nearby,
followed the sound along
with a Dragonfly.

I removed my slippers to feel.
The tickling grass on my toes,
I bent down to smell the lovely

Flowers with my nose.

I could now see the beautiful
Stream flow,
I sat down and immersed my
Feet in its water, which felt
Icy cold,
And saw the dew drops on
The grass blades glow.

Then I realized my heart felt
younger,
no matter I was how old!

19. Strangers

A Poem

We, Strangers
You and I
Walk in the Streets
See each other
Sometimes we smile
Sometimes, we don't
Sometimes we talk
Sometimes, we don't
We are so much alike
Yet, for each other
we are unknown

We mask our feelings
Behind our cold faces
Sometimes we open
ourselves to others
as though we are
best of friends
Yes, It's two strangers
Who could become
close friends
close foes too

It's strangers
who strangely
meet and fall
in love too
It's strangers just

like you and I
Who makes people
People make nations
Nation's world

We, Strangers
come together
in a hotel
Sip cups of tea
We travel together
on land, air and sea

We come together
under one single
Umbrella

in the rain

We don't know
the game of
the divine
Whether this is
our first and
last meeting
or we'll meet
once again.

20. Believe

A Poem

There won't be any sunshine.
In the darkness and pain,
But darkness and pain
Will not forever remain.

That's what you should
Always believe in.
There won't be any brightness.
In the darkest hour,
Even the candlelight could
Be blown off by the wind.

That doesn't mean that
Brightness won't come
Back again.
Hold courage and
Determination in
Your heart and soul,
And move ahead
Without giving up
Towards your goal.

Things do change as
The time passes by,
And you can make
The difference is if you do try.
Always believe in
Yourself and never

Ever give up, my friend
And you'll surely
Succeed in the end.

The ascend of the Mountain
would be very steep
and challenging,
But you would come
Down the other
Side of success
With much ease.

Everything appears
Impossible unless
You do try.
Falling doesn't matter,

When you'll surely
Touch the sky.

Only then will you realize
Nothing is impossible
As the time goes by.
Pick up your reason
To believe in,
And try it as would
Normally do,
You'll surely achieve
What you set
Out to achieve.

21. I

A Poem

When I fall,
I stand up.
When I fail,
I don't give up.

When I lose,
Still, I hope.
In sufferings,
I try to cope.

When I'm lost,
I find myself.

When reality
Deceives,
Yet I dream.

In pain,
I try to smile.
In success,
I let go of my tears.

In sharing,
I find my joy.
In this life,
I'm a winded toy.

In strangers,
I seek attachment.
In life,

I seek detachment.

In fear,
I find my courage.
When I despair,
Yet I believe.

In anger,
I maintain cool.
I know I'm
Nothing,
Yet I try to
Be something.

22. The Unspoken Tree

A Poem

I would like you to see
My tree of life
Which has grown so big
So broad, you see

Would you like to have
Some fruits, my friend
Let me tell you some
Of them are sour
And they remind my
Sorrows and pain

Some of my fruits

Are sweet too

Reminding my cheer

And happiness

The green leaves remind

The days of my life

The fallen leaves

Are my memories

I would go the day

The last leaf breaks

I'd stood tall on

My roots and achieved

Things in this limited

Space provided to me

Every tree has some
Story to tell
But unfortunately
We are destined to be
Unspoken, you see.

23. The More I See You

A Poem

The more I see you
The better it makes me feel
You are like a fantasy
In this world of so real

Your smile makes me forget
All my sorrows and pain
I wish this smile on your
face would forever remain

You are like the glow of
the candle in the darkness

O, wind, please don't blow
off the glow till the end

The more I see you
The better it makes me feel
You are like a dream
In this world of so real
Please don't wake me up
As I don't want this dream to
end.

24. Spring

A Poem

Welcome Spring
The cold winter
Is now past
And dead
Even the rain
Had his days
Of glory
And has now gone

The birds sing
In chorus
And some alone

On the branches
Of the green trees
Which winter had
Once possessed

The sun smiles
In the sky, with
His beautiful shine
Bringing colour
And beauty to
All the things
Created by divine
You dress in nature
such that she
Appears even more
Pretty

See the joy on
The turtle's face
Those beautiful
Flowers sway
In grace

Listen to the
Wonderful song
Of the flowing
Stream
I can't see so
Much beauty
Even in my dream.

* 9 7 8 9 3 6 9 5 3 4 0 4 3 *